Measuring at School

By Nick Rebman

level
1
little blue readers

www.littlebluehousebooks.com

Little Blue House is distributed by North Star Editions:
sales@northstareditions.com | 888-417-0195

Produced for Little Blue House by Red Line Editorial.

Photographs ©: Shutterstock Images, cover, 7 (pencil), 7 (ruler), 8–9 (books), 9 (girl), 15, 16 (top left), 16 (top right), 16 (bottom left), 16 (bottom right); iStockphoto, 4, 11, 12–13

Library of Congress Control Number: 2020900799

ISBN
978-1-64619-166-6 (hardcover)
978-1-64619-200-7 (paperback)
978-1-64619-268-7 (ebook pdf)
978-1-64619-234-2 (hosted ebook)

Printed in the United States of America
Mankato, MN
012021

About the Author

Nick Rebman enjoys reading, walking his dog, and traveling to places where he doesn't speak the language. He lives in Minnesota.

Table of Contents

Measuring at School

We use a ruler.

We measure the boy.

We use a ruler.

We measure the pencil.

pencil

We use a ruler.

We measure the books.

We use a ruler.

We measure the wood.

We use a ruler.

We measure the bone.

bone

We use a ruler.

We measure the plant.

plant

Glossary

books

ruler

plant

wood

Index